Introduction

Within the pages of this book are descriptions of real encounters that have been documented and reports of real creatures, monsters or mysterious beings that people have actually seen. Even though there are many more exciting and interesting creatures throughout the planet I only focused on the ones within the USA.

I did not list regular type animals that science could explain or list in the catalog of normal life or species. The only time I did was when the creature that could fall under the category like the other monsters.

You will read about many unique and mysterious beings or creatures that seem to defy the laws of nature or are possible new forms of life that science has yet to explain. Some of these creatures fall beyond the laws of science.

I myself have had my own share of encounters with beings and creatures that are unexplainable. Those personal encounters I will not mention in this book. I can say however that when a person witnesses first hand something that goes beyond our world of understanding it can leave an imprint on ones that life forever.

The cases and reports mentioned are from actual real document reports.

Everything in this book is listed by state in alphabetical order for a quick and easy reference guide.

Maybe this will influence you to take up an adventurous quest into the unknown in search of seeing one of the creatures listed here.

Perhaps one day someone will be able to catch one of these creatures, gather information, or even take a good clear photo and prove the existence of one of these exciting life forms that are with us on this planet.

Alabama

Choccolocca Monster

In the late 1960's there was a sighting of mysterious creature. It terrified many people and stories grew around Choccolocca about this creature.

As time went on this became a popular legend. It wasn't until October 2001 there was an article written in the Anniston Star newspaper which revealed that the creature in fact a local resident, Neal Williamson. He had dressed in a cow skull and a sheet at the time as a teenager. He would put on his costume and jump out of the woods at roadside or run across the road and startle motorists. People at the time were very frightened of this and even the very talk of the creature that other accounts were linked to it.

Supposedly on one night when he jumped out from behind a bush and did a little dance or routine that he normally did to frighten drivers, a truck had stopped. When it did the driver leaped out with a shot gun and opened fire. Neal ran into the woods and through some barbed wire. This scared him so bad that he decided not to do it ever again. But the rumors of the creature continued over the years until the truth finally came out.

Trisckers

There are many legends with the Native Americans in Alabama. They consist of tales of people that can transform from humans to animals at will as well as beings that are able to "trick" others into doing things for them. Such as giving up their possessions to doing what ever is asked. It is said that to beat a trickster you must continue to ask questions before doing something. For a trickster will lose interest with you when you do this.

Wolf Woman
In the early 1970's there were reports of a beautiful woman that was part human and part wolf. She is said that the top half from the waist up was a very sexy woman but the rest of the body resembled a wolf that walked up right like a person. The body was covered in hair. More than 50 people have claimed to have seen her.

White Thang
In the 1940's people reported seeing a creature that was approximately seven feet tall. It was covered in white hair. When it would let out a scream that sounded like a female screaming. However, some have said that it sounded like a panther. Some have speculated that this creature was actually a large albino bear. After the 40's reports of this creature have calmed down. Some believed that it went into hibernation and will one day awaken returning to the areas of Morgan, Etowah, and Jefferson.

The Metal Man

On the night of October 17, 1973 report was called into the police station by a   shaken resident of falkville about a space that had landed in the field. The chief of police believed what he had heard and quickly headed out with his camera around 10 pm.

When he arrived there was no spaceship but a being dressed in a silver type metal. It was very smooth and shiny, almost like liquid metal.

As he pulled up the being was caught in his headlights and began to run. As it did he pursed reaching speeds up 35 miles an hour across the rough terrain. The being ran faster than his police cruiser. Disappearing into the night. There were no further reports of this being. Maybe it went back to its ship or it was also believed that it could have shed its metal shell and is still wandering Alabama

Alaska
Iliamna Lake Monster

The Iliamna Lake monster is commonly referred to by the locals as Illie. It's legend has haunted the Alaskan fishing village of Iliamna. It roams the waters of the area. It is said that it has a square head which is used for ram into boats. The size is said to range from 10 to 30 feet long. There have been deaths reported to this creature but there have yet to be any real proof of it.

Ice Monster
There have been recent reports of an unusual creature that has been spotted and even filmed in the Chena River, in Fairbanks. Some have called it the Ice Monster. There have been some that have claimed it to be a new form of crocodile. It seems to hide under clumps of ice and move underneath these clumps like a crocodile.
Nothing has been proven yet because it is still under investigation.

Blood Sucking Ice Worm
Ice worms are common in Alaska. They are black worms that live in ice and have been known to burrow into icebergs. Normally they are harmless but there is a legend amongst some fishermen that there is an ice worm that feeds on blood. They have been said to get into a fishermen's clothing or boots and burrow into their skin only to eat them alive.

Disappearances in Nome
There have been reports of thousands people just disappearing without a trace from the time period of the early 1960's until 2004. There could have been earlier disappearances that have not been recorded. No one knows what happened to these people. It was once believed to have been a serial killer or due to the harsh climate. However, most believe that the disappearances are because of UFO's and are being abducted. There are some that have reported seeing a being that is human shaped shadow and have pulled them into another dimension.

Arkansas

Gowrow

Gowrow is a giant lizard, said to live in caves of Arkansas (Boone and Searcy Counties, northern Arkansas). It has two tusks on its head and is 20ft in length.It Makes an assortment of groans and hisses. Sometime before 1935, E. J. Rhodes heard a commotion in a deep cavern called Devil's Hole, 3 miles northwest of Myrtle, Arkansas. He crawled down 200 feet to investigate, but couldn't see anything. Later, when he lowered a flatiron on a rope into the cavern, something bit through the rope.

Ozark Howler
The Howler has been reported to be a great cat, or dog, or bear-like beast with eyes that glow red from behind a black pelt. The monster stands four-feet-tall at the shoulder, and some witnesses say the beast has horns.

White River Monster
Named Whitey for its home in the White River, this gray-skinned river monster first appeared in 1915. A local plantation owner who saw Whitey in 1937 said it looked about five feet wide, twelve feet long, and had the face of a catfish
Witnesses saw a twenty-foot-long gray monster with a horn and spiny back in the river in 1971. Investigators discovered fourteen-inch, three-toed tracks of a large animal that apparently emerged from the river, and walked on the shore, crushing brush, and breaking small trees. Hundreds of people have claimed to see Whitey over the years.
Since 1973, Whitey has been protected by law

Fouke

The Fouke Monster is also known as the Boggy Creek Monster.
It is approximately 7 feet tall, weighing 300 to 500 pounds. Dark
brown hair covers entire body. Dark colored skin and has an
ape-like face. First sighting was in 1908 and the continues to be
sight to this day. There have yet to be any photos taken of this
creature but have found tracks.
In the early 1970's the newspaper accounts brought this creature
worldwide fame. And even created a movie based on the
information.

Arizona

Mogollon Monster
The mogollon monster is reported to be over 7 feet tall and have super human strength. Has large red wild looking eyes. The body is covered in long black hair but during the summer months the hair is supposedly reddish brown. Covering its entire massive and muscular body including its face. Similar to the description of the Big foot. Is said to have an odor that smells of dead fish or a swamp.
When it walks it takes large strides and leaves behind large foot prints that have measured 22 inches in length. It will emit a loud blood curdling scream like a woman in distress when either fearful or when angered.
It has been seen near Payson and Whiteriver. There have also been a few sightings near the fort apache Indian reservation. Even though there have been sightings there have been no accounts of any killings or missing persons that have been linked with it.
This has been the object of spooky campfire tales over the years.

Werewolves
It has been reported that there packs of werewolves in Springerville Arizona. Werewolves are much larger than regular wolves and walk up right on their hind legs like a person.
They are said to move silently and glowing red eye's. If they spot a person they will run after them. There have been several accounts of injuries credited to these creatures.
Dogs are able to pick up their scent and will start barking right away or go after them. Most dogs will not return if they attack these wolves.

Thunderbird

It is said that in tombstone there are large birds. Some larger than cars. There is a story about two cowboys in 1890 that encountered one of these birds and shot it. The head looks like an alligator and the body is smooth like a serpent. It measured 92 inches long.

Gomphother
A Gomphothere is a distant relative to elephants with broad snouts and elongated jaws similar to a crocodile. They were found in North America over 12 to 2 million years ago and were around 9 feet tall with two or four tusks. The bones of these ancient animals have been found in the southern portion of Arizona near the Mexico border. They are believed to have vanished around the time humans started roaming the Earth.

Dust Creatures
Throughout Arizona there are reports of Dust like creatures that appear in the desert. Legends state that these are devils at play. But if you encounter these creatures they have been know to injure people physically and cause sickness

Supernatural beings and Aliens
There are several reports of Supernatural beings, beings from other dimensions, and aliens in Sedona Arizona. So many reports there have been books written just on them.
It is believed that there are inter-dimensional gateways in various locations throughout Sedona. According to legend this was an area for the Gods and no human was suppose to live there. But now it is a thriving community and almost everyone living there can tell you a story or two about strange encounters in that area.

Devil

Devil spotted in Tucson Arizona. Images of this being have been posted all over the internet about a shadowy winged creature. So far it has only been seen by one man and he took a photo of this creature. Nothing else is known about it at this time but is something to keep a look out for.

California

Bigfoot
The stories of Bigfoot are many and have been reported for years. It has been seen in most of Northern California. It is described as large hairy humanoid type creature. It stands between 6 and 9 feet. It is said to have a strong unpleasant smell. Foot prints left behind have measured 24 inches long and 8 inches wide. Physical evidence has been lift behind along with several photos to validate the sightings.

Billiwhack Monster
The creature is said to have the body of a man but the head and horns of a goat with long claws. Its body very muscular due to its strength. It calls Camulos Ranch its home and has been encountered on Wheeler canyon road. Seen carrying a club or stick.
There are several reports of this creature attacking people in 1964. Mostly teenagers encountered the creature. One belief was that it was around their age and seeking companionship. However when it encountered people things did not go well. It threw rocks at cards and people. These reports have grown. Believed by many to be the results of a scientific experiment that has gone wrong and the creature escaped its lab. It was part of an experiment to create super soldiers. But they experimented on orphaned children and teenagers.
Some believe that it has mated with a human female and she gave birth to it's offspring. It is not known if she survived after giving birth.
In the same area in 1939 several people reported seeing a creature the size of a twelve year old boy that had long arms and looked like it was half monkey. After these sightings they seem to calm down until the goat like creatures that started to appear in the 60's.

Tahquitz
A mysterious evil spirit that will stalk its victims during the day
and sometimes torment them with fear only to devour them
when the sun goes down. Trapping their souls with it for all
eternity.
It is said to haunt the San Jacinto mountain range or Palm
Springs.

Lizard people
It is not known where they come from but they are to believed
to either alien or from a lost civilization that we do not know
about. They are believed to live within Mount Shasta and are
highly advanced race of beings. Only a handful of people have
seen these beings and some have even said to have
communicated with them.
They have a humanoid body but look like lizards and they wear
unusual clothing that is unlike any seen before.
Many people believe that there are some that resemble human
features but have eyes and tongues like a lizard. They wear
contacts to keep their identity a secret and are now living
beyond California.

Pier Serpents
In various parts of California at the base of the piers reports of
strange black serpents live in the waters and in the sand. Attach
themselves to the ankles and legs of those that walk around the
area. They feed on blood.

Lone Mountain Pine Devil
Also called the California Mountain devil. Is described as being
a large creature with a humanoid body that is covered in black
fur, has large wings, claws, and venomous fangs. This creature
is said to feast on the wicked and can sense or "Know" their
sins. Tearing their bodies apart and leaving only pieces.

Stories of this creature started in the 1800's when people started discovering body parts. Even though the creature is said to only attract the wicked, it has also killed innocent people. It is thought it did this out of   hunger .

Wild eye Joe
There is rumor of a man that is some sort of being. Not sure if he is alive or spirit. He looks like a vagrant with messed up hair and has a crazy look in his eyes. He goes up to people and just says wild gibberish that does not make sense while waving his hands in the air. Then will shuffle past and when you turn around he is gone.
He is sometimes just seen at morning hours just before the sun rises walking the beach then vanishing.

Hollywood tormented souls
There are numerous sightings of spirits on the Hollywood blvd. one of the most popular is of young man that will be standing on the side of the road or waving at a car but when the car drives past or pulls up next to him he vanishes into thin air. It is believed that he is haunting the streets where he worked as a male prostitute. His name is not known. It is said that he is body was found on a side street in the 70's with no id and was labeled as a john doe.
Another is known as switch blade sally. She is a black woman with an afro. She is seen in the alley ways off of Hollywood blvd or the in the shadows. She is not known if she is a spirit or some other type of being. She has been known to stable men with switch blade when then become rough with a woman they are with. After she stabs them she vanishes. She has also been known to take things from people.

Silde - Rock Bolter
a bizarre creature recounted by the lumberjacks of North America during the 19th and early 20th centuries. It is believed to live in the mountains of Colorado, but this beast only lived in the mountains where the slope was more than a 45 degree angle. It has an immense head, with small eyes, and large mouth. It has a fluked tail like a dolphin, with enormous grab-hooks.
All day long this creature will just wait for a tourist or helpless creature below it. At the right moment, it will lift its tail, thus loosening its hold on the mountain, and descend rapidly down the slope. With the beast's mouth wide open it would swallow all that got in its way. Whole parties of tourists are reported to have been gulped up in one scoop by taking parties far back into the hills. Its body is also so large and strong that trees in its path are broken and destroyed. Its own impetus carries it up the next slope, where it again slaps its tail over the ridge and waits.

Vampires
Strange reports of Vampires have taken place from the 1800's until today. Reports cover the entire state of Colorado. Both male and female.

Dinosaurs
Residents of Pueblo have claim to have seen Tyrannosaurus-Rex type dinosaurs moving along the country side. The Creature is said to be about three feet tall, powerful hind legs, tiny front legs and a long tail

Strange shadows

In the mountains of Aspen and Vail there have been talks of people seeing things in the darkness or the shadows. They have said that then shadows seem to move like they are alive. Living darkness. People have been overwhelmed with emotions or sadness after seeing these shadows. They have a fear of shadows will consume them. I was not able to find any information about people vanishing because of shadows in Colorado.

Connecticut

  Melon heads - Melon heads are the names given the creatures that have the bodies of humans but have oversized heads that resemble melons. These humanoid creatures are known to hide and emerge to attack anyone that is nearby or considered a threat.

These creatures are not just in Connecticut but there are reports of them in Ohio and Michigan.

There is one theory about the melon head origins is that there were a couple of patients from a mental that escaped into the woods and then mated with females. These females produced wild mentally unstable mutant type people.

Another theory is that they are just a different form of people that are deformed and live in the woods.

Then there is the wild theory that they are either descendants of Aliens that crashed on this planet and mated with humans. Or just a wild creature of the forest.

The Winsted Wildman - Similar to big foot. This creature is described as having the body of a male, over six feet tall, having a males face, brawny, and covered with thick hair all over this is body as well as his face. If he had no hair that covered his entire body he would resemble an ordinary man.

The legend started in 1895 and reports continued until the 70's before dropping out of sight. It is not believed to be the same creature but some how descendants of the original creature. The one that was last seen in the 1974 was described the same way except was much larger and taller, believed to be around 300 pounds.

There were no mentions of it harming any one, only scaring those that seen him. But the creature also became fearful as after coming close to a human would run away and vanish into the woods.

<u>The Makiawisug of the Mohegan Hill </u>- The little people. It is
said that the Nakiawisug are good creatures that are to be
treated with kindness. For if you do they will grant you a
special gift or favor. They are said to also having special healing
powers for they know the mysterious powers of plants.
They are small no taller than a persons knee but most are much
smaller. They are believed to have be adorned in brightly
colored flowers, gemstones, and colorful fabrics.
It is said that if you make eye contact with them or stare at them
it is considered rude and impolite. If you should they will point
their finger at you and cause you to freeze in place. When this
happens they will take all of your possessions including your
clothing. Leaving you naked in the woods. Until you unfreeze
hours later.
However, Showing them respect they will repay you with
precious gifts.

Delaware

Mhuwe
Mhuwe also known as the Windigo. It is a large hairy beast that feasts on human flesh. It is said that these creatures were once humans that consumed human flesh and this turned them into monsters. There is another legend that states that if you give one of these creatures fruit to eat it will turn them back into a human losing all memory of their former lives as monsters.

Zwannendael Merman
A foot long creature that is on display in the Zwannendael Museum is said to be a Merman that was captured by a member of the Lewis family that was a sea captain.

Bigfoot
There are a couple of reports of a Bigfoot type creature being spotted in Sussex county. A tall muscular man like creature covered in hair all over its body have been seen. Reports have only seen the creature briefly and disappear into woods.

Florida

Skunk ape
The skunk ape, is also known as the Swamp Cabbage man, Stink Ape, Swamp ape, Louisianan Bigfoot, Myakka ape, and Swampsquatch, it is a humanoid type creature that is said to inhabit the state of Florida. The reason its name is that it has an unpleasant odor that is said to accompany it as well as leave the scent behind were ever it goes.
Sightings of this creature were common in the 1960's and continue on to this day. Reports from being attacked by the creature to a woman who claims that apples are being taken from her trees in her yard. There are many reports from fearful people that say the creature attacked them and try to kill them while other people say that creature is a gently creature just trying to survive. Even though these reports vary the only thing that it really has in common is foul smell that surrounds it. It is said that you smell the beast before you see it or know that it is around.

Reptile men
In the swampy regions of Florida there have been reports of half man half reptile creatures. It is said that a woman gave birth in the swamp and the swamp turned the baby into this creature. But it does not account for the many sightings.

Lake Clinch Monster
Lake Clinch in Polk county has a long history of a serpent like monster living in its depths.

It is said to be 30 feet long, have a hump back, long neck and flippers. Reports of this creature started in 1876 til modern time. However, the creature seems to be of different colors in today's reports compared to the earlier account. When it was first sighted it was said to be green and black. The more modern sightings the creature is a yellow and green.

Muck Monster
The Much monster is a serpent-like creature that has been seen in Lake worth lagoon. It is said to be ten feet long.

Sauropod Dinosaur
Sightings of this creature began in 1961 to the present day. People have claimed to have seen a dinosaur type creature on the banks of the water.

Chupacabra type creature
A creature with long claws, red eye's, and fangs, some have even seen it with wings. This creature is said to be fierce.

Bermuda Beings
At the tip of the Bermuda triangle that reaches the shores of the Florida and Miami area, it is said that there is an entrance where other worldly beings and even creatures will enter.
There have been many reports and cases about the mysterious Bermuda triangle where people have disappeared. But what only a select few know is that even though people are said to vanish in this triangle as well as having strange visions of unusual sites, that this doorway of where things vanish there is also a doorway where things are said to appear.

It is not known if these beings are actually from the triangle but they are said to have been seen near where the triangle reaches land. These beings are said to look like people but they have a bluish cast to their skins and wear unusual metallic type clothing. They seem to Shift through dimensions. Their eyes glow. Reports of time disruption have been noted.
It is not known where they actually come from or where they go but they are seen in the surrounding area.

Zombie like Creatures
In modern times there have been reports of zombies or the undead walking all over parts of Florida. It is believed that the Government is keeping this a secret because when one is seen or discovered it is either quickly captured or killed and all traces are covered up.

Georgia

Raptor type creature spotted in the Georgia woods. Reports have said that it resembles a dinosaur type creature. Unusual sounds are not uncommon in the Woods. But there is a special sound that creature makes and it seems to draw people to investigate and when they spot this creature they run.

Altamaha-ha

Around the areas of Darien and Butler island there is a popular belief a sea creature. It is said to resemble the Lock Ness. Reports started around the 18th century and continue to this day.

It is said to swim like a dolphin. Have very large eye's and a snout like a crocodile with large teeth and a grayish green serpent like body that measures 20 to 30 feet long.

The creature has been spotted basking itself on the shores or moving casually along the edges of the rivers only to return back into the waters.

The creature has only known to attack if it feels threatened by someone or something. If you remain calm and don't move it will just move past you.

Hawaii

Night marchers - In Hawaiian legend it is said that the night marchers are a band of deadly ghosts of Hawaiian warriors. The are said to come forth from their burial grounds or rise up out of the sea in groups near sacred spaces. They are said to make their appearances sometimes during religious ceremonies or during important times when protection is needed for those that are in need on Hawaii. These warriors are said to vanish leaving no traces of them even being there.

Menehune - this being is very similar to a leprechaun. Their size range from the size that can fit in the palm of your hand to two feet tall. They are said to be both playful and master builders. They were believed by some to live on the Islands before they were forced to go into hiding. When people see them they seem to fall into a trance that will put them into a sleep. They do not speak a known language but they do speak with their minds and can use this mind power to gain control over others when needed.

They are said to live in clumps of trees or in caves. They resemble humanoid type figures with large eyes and pointed ears.

Reports of these creatures have been made since people started living on the islands.

Mokuhinia - A large Dragon like creature is said to roam the islands and living in the remote pools. One such large dragon appeared before a crown of over a thousand people in 1838 and continue to this day to have sightings.

Mu - A water vampire type water creature. It is said to look like a human but with large fangs. It is naked and lives in the waters. It will either grab someone and drag them into the water or lure them seductively. Once in the water they will pull them under and while the person is drowning they will drink their blood.
These creatures cannot live above the water. Like in vampire legends where they cannot be in sunlight these creatures cannot be in the light but they also cannot be out of the water. They are said to sleep in underwater caves or in the ground below the water.

Idaho

Paddler - Another lake monster. This creature is said to be 20 to 40 feet long and resembles a large serpent. It is said to reside in Lake Pend.

Water Babies - there is an ancient native american legend about small child like creatures that are living around the rocks near the waters of Idaho. These children are said to be trickster type entities that have only one goal and that is to murder anyone that they encounter. It is said that anyone that comes in contact with these creatures will not survive.

Bear Lake Monster - The legend of the Bear Lake monster is said to have been started by a colonizer of the area. He stated that within the water lies a Water Devil. This devil is massive in size and will kill who ever it chooses.

Illinois

Enfield Horror - This legend began in a small town of Enfield in 1973. Reports began that year of a creature that is short about 3 to 5 feet tall, has two arms that have hands with claws, three legs, an oddly shaped head and a muscular body. This creature is said to have extraordinary strength. It has been linked to all sorts of problems in the town that range from scratches on buildings to injuring others. There have been some people that believe that creature only comes close to civilization in search of food and it only harms accidentally when it tries to flee with it is afraid.
Many believe it is an Alien while others believe it to be some sort of demon. But many just believe it is some sort of mutant.

Large Black Cat - Panthers of Illinois - there have been many unusual sightings of a large black cat the some believe to panthers that roam the neighborhood of Roscoe Village.

Murphysboro Mud Monster - Also called Big Muddy. A hairy, smelly humanoid type creature that stands seven feet tall and is covered in mud. It is said to have white madded fur but because it is so covered in mud that it has hard to see the white fur. Sounds of an inhuman cry are projected from the creature. Some believe this is done out of fear or loneliness while others said it gives off the cry before it attacks its victims.

Thunderbirds - Starting in 1948 reports of very large birds. These birds range in size from the size of a condor to that of airplane. In 1977, two of these birds are said to have attacked a group of children and one of the children was picked up by one of the birds. He was carried about 35 feet before dropping the child because it was frightened off by the child's mother. The rumors of these large birds continue to this day and now a days being shrugged off as a hoax.

Indiana

Beast of Busco is a large snapping turtle. Once feared is now a calm creature that now goes by the name of Oscar and lives quietly on a farm.

Werewolves - reports and sightings of large werewolf type creatures are said to roam various parts of Indiana. They are said to resemble wolves that walk upright on their hind legs. Covered in thick black hair. They are said to howl and when they do, it sends chills their your body.

Creature of Mt Baldy - Mt Baldy is a large sand dune known as a living dune because it will continue to grow over time. People seem to be drawn to this area for recreational activities. It is rumored that there is an unknown creature that lives within this sand dune and has been known to pull people into the sands. The creature is also believed to be responsible for the mysterious holes and tunnels within the dunes that also cause people to slip under the sand.

Iowa

Van Meter - In 1903, in the small town of Van Meter a giant bat like creator came out of an old abandoned mine. Several residents reported seeing a half human with large bat like wings flying around. It moved in speeds that were faster than anything at the time. There was a powerful and terrible stench that was emitted from it. The creature had horns on it's head and between those horns a bright light would shine from it. This light could cause temporary blindness by those that would look at it directly. Some of the witnesses have said that it resembled the shape and body of a devil.

People have reported more than one of these creatures. The actual last true sighting of the creatures was when the town people went after it and when they approached what they thought was one creature was actually two. One large one and one smaller one. Both creatures vanished into a ball of light. None of these creatures were seen again however other strange supernatural encounters have been taken place in that town since that time.

Mysterious Phantom Kangaroos -   Starting in 1999, there have been reports of people seeing Kangaroo type creatures in various parts of Iowa. They would disappear as quickly as people would see them.

Kansas

Beaman Beast - In 1904, a circus train derailed and many of the animals escaped. One of the animals was a 12 foot gorilla. It is believed that this gorilla mated with something else and created a hybrid creature that haunts various farms and wooded areas. However, no evidence was actually collected. Only sightings have been reported.

Sinkhole Sam - Lake Inman, is the home to this creature. It is said to resemble a large earthworm. 15 feet long. It has been seen in burrowing into the nearby earth and moving through the water.

Creek Creatures - There have been some reports of a small creatures with tentacles that live in the creeks. They will move quickly through the waters and then burrow into the mud or hide under rocks. Some have said these creatures have moved around them and even touch them when in the waters but none have been actually seen or captured.

Mysterious portal lights - This is not a creature but I thought it was worth mention. In parts of Kansas people have seen unusual lights in the sky and in some cases close to the ground. These circles seem to be portals because odd shaped beings have been seen coming out of those circle of lights for just a brief moment and then step back inside. Then once they go back into these lights they would vanish or go dark.

Kentucky

Pope Lick Monster - Legendary being that is said to reside under the bridge of Pope Lick creek in Louisville. This being is said to be that of a half beast and half human. It has the body of a human and the head of a goat. It has long horns and dirty brown hair. Has been seen carrying an axe like weapon. Said to have hypnotic powers and put people into a trance, making them do what ever it wants. The being also can mimic a persons voice and lure many of its victims onto the bridge to be hit by the on coming train. Many believe that it is a mistreated side show freak and is seeking revenge for its unfair treatment.

Werewolf of Breeding - Recent sightings of werewolves have been reported in Breeding. People have claimed to have seen large wolf type creatures and then turn into humans while they run through the trees. They have not harmed anyone one yet.

Goblins - For over 50 years people have been reporting goblin type creatures. The sightings begin in 1955 in Kelly and Hopkinsville in Christian county. In the beginning it was shrugged off as a silver painted monkey. But there are more than one. Reports are now made over the entire state even to this day.

  These creatures are silver to black in color. They have the body of human with a extremely large head with equally large ears and long fingers. Some reports have said that these creatures have glowing eyes. Approximately 4 feet tall.
Many believe these creatures are survivors of an alien ship that crashed while others believe that they are from some unknown dimension.

Louisiana

Honey Island Swamp Monster - The first reports of this creature was made in 1963. It is said to be humanoid in shape, 7 feet tall, have long hair over its entire body, and have only three web toes. The creature lives in the swamps. Tours continue daily to visit the area where the creature lives in hopes of catch a glimpse. Out side of it scaring people there are no reports of this creature hurting anyone. But will attack if scared or feel threatened.

Momo creature - In 1971, it was reported that a creature with a large pumpkin like head with a human body that had thick black fur coverings humanoid body and eyes. It is said to travel up and down the Mississippi river. People have said that they could smell a terrible odor before they seen it. This creature is known to go after small animals and mainly dogs to eat. No one knows if it has eaten any humans yet.

Vampires and Vampire like beings - Even before many books TV shows and movies have made the subject of vampires popular, it is said that in Louisiana has a large population of these supernatural beings. They range from normal looking human type beings that no one would be able to tell the difference to boney undead zombie like creatures that feast on the blood of the living. The ones that resemble humans tend to hold normal jobs and keep to themselves. Where as the other zombie like creatures were only seen at night near graveyards and swamps.

Supernatural Swamp beings - All types of creatures and beings have been spotted in the swamps of Louisiana. They are said to even be home to many spirits. Some believe it is the swamps themselves that have the power to create these beings while others believe they are doorways to the other worlds.

Maine

Pocomoonshine monster - Sightings for this lake monster have been reported since 1873.   Lake Nesiek is the home to this creature. Its body to that of a 40 foot long serpent. It starts out as just a ripple on the water then it emerges. It is said to appear mainly at night or at sunset but it has made an appearance during the daylight hours.

Argopelter - A fierce creature. The body is said to similar to an ape but with long arms. It lives in the hollow of trees. It is believed to throw things either from the hollow or tops of trees at people that walk near by. If this start to happens, you are to run quickly out of that area. It tries to knock its victim out or kill it and then devour the entire body.
People that have vanished mysteriously have been linked to this creature.

White bigfoot - In the forests of Maine, reports of a white Bigfoot type creature have been made in recent years. It is not known where it came from. Some have said that it comes down from Canada. Recent reports have spotted the creature recently in Eddington.
It is believed to be over 7 feet tall, have the body of a man, and covered with long thick white hair.

Maryland

Goatman - There are several stories behind this creature. Here are just the top three. One is believed that he is an experiment that has gone wrong which was done at the Beltsville research agricultural center that created him. Another story is that of a goat herder that loved his goats so much that he lost his mind when some teenagers killed his animals. And there is that this creature is actually some sort of supernatural being.

It is half man and half goat. Has the body of a male but has the head of a goat. Some reports say that he has human feet while others say they resemble a goats hoof. Stands approximately six feet tall.   Has defined physical features and is naked. Yells, howlers, and makes goat sounds.
He has been known to terrorize lovers in parked cars at lovers lane or other areas near the tree's or woods by peering into the windows to watch them. Sometimes pressing his face against the window or scratching the outside of the car with his fingers. Chased teenagers. Decapitates dogs, usually when the dogs go after him.
His appearance has been around since the 60's. Some believed that he mated with a human female and his offspring is the one that is being seen today.

Phantom Blue dog of Rose Hill - As the legend goes, In the 1700's Charles Thomas Sims and his faithful dog drank in a tavern one night, drunkenly and loudly boasting of his wealth in gold. He was slyly led out of the tavern by Henry Hanos who took him to Rose Hill where he was beaten to death by Hanos and his gang. Sims' loyal dog tried defending his master and ultimately died as well. Hanos then gathered the gold and buried it under a holly tree that was along Rose Hill road. When Hanos went back to retrieve his treasure, he was supposedly frightened away by the ghost of a large blue dog. He suddenly fell ill and died a few days later.
It is said that every February 8th the dog will return to the very spot where his own died.

Snallygaster - In 1909, it is said that a giant dragon like creature attacked many people and even a train. It was said to have enormous wings, steel like claws, one eye, and the body of a dragon. After its few encounters it was never seen or mentioned again.

Chessie - A serpent like creature very similar to the loch Ness monsters has been reported to be seen in the Chesapeake Bay. It is said to be between 25 and 40 feet long. Has a dark snake like body and even move like a snake through the waters.
Has been known to bump into sea vessels in the water.

Massachusetts

Pukwudgie - The Pukwudgie is a small creature that stands between 2 and 3 feet tall. It has grey skin with large eye's and ears. Some have seen spikes like a porcupine for hair that go down its back while others say it is a thick hair that resembles spikes. It has a humanoid type body but with a long face and teeth. They are said to wear clothing that appears to be hand made by them. They live in the woods and near cliffs. They have been known to scare people in the woods and chase them for sport. As well as pushing people over cliffs or into on coming traffic and other methods. These creatures seem to take pleasure in the terror of others.

There are some of these creatures that are said to glow at night or in the dark.

It is believed that these creatures have been around since before any humans lived in north American. Some believe them to be part of the fairy family.

Michigan

Dogman - The Michigan Dogman was first witnessed in 1887 and continues to this day. In Wexford County, Michigan the Dogman is described as being seven feet tall, Blue eyes (sometimes seen with Amber eye's that glow) dog like face on a human head, resemble a dog but the body of a man, canine muscular legs, tail, and with a torso that is crossed between a human and an animal. Said to give off a howl that is both a wolf and a human screaming.
The Dogman appears ever ten years and falls on years that end in the number seven. Sightings have been reported all over Michigan. There is even a song that has been written about it.

Dewey Lake Monster - The sightings began in 1964 in Dowagiac, Michigan. It is said to reside in the Lake itself. Witnesses have said that it stands ten feet tall, Similar to Bigfoot descriptions, the body is covered in hair, cone shaped head, bear like webbed claws for hands as well as feet, and has a humanoid shape body. Reports of people missing in the area are linked to this creature and the lake. There have been eyewitnesses that have had their cars either clawed up by the creature or flipped over.

Corn Man - In Isabella county and other various parts of the rural county Michigan, reports of a being that lives in the corn have been seen. He is said to be five feet tall and resemble a shadow. It moves through the corn. Witness have seen it reach out to try and grab them. People have said that they have an explained overwhelming sensation of fear and anxiety before seeing this being, as if some type of energy is being projected over them just before they see it.

Ridgeway Monster - In 1986 in the town of Ridgeway near Tecumseh started the reports of this creature. It is said to have a humanoid shape body that is covered in red hair. Has glowing green eyes. Long fingers and nails. Said to peer into the windows of homes in this area and watch people from the brush. Missing items from homes and yards are attributed to this creature. No reports of anyone being harmed. This creature is said to be timid.

Minnesota

Wendigo - One of the most dangerous monsters in America. The name of this creature means, "Evil that Devours". It is a cannibalistic creatures. Said to once be human but that became possessed by an evil demon which forced them to eat human flesh. Once they devour this flesh it transforms them into these creatures forever. Forcing them to roam in search of more victims. These creatures have been sighted in the Great lakes area as well and   similar creatures in the northern forests of the Atlantic coast.

Some believe that it started in the early days during a harsh winter and there was no food. People began to eat each other and the dead to survive. This cannibalistic act brought forth a demon which changed them into these creatures. Since that day, the demon will roam the area for those that fill themselves with such greed in thinking of only themselves and then transform them. It is also said that if one of these creatures should bite or scratch you then you can be transformed that way.

The wendigo will start out in human form but then after the transformation will become w beast that sometimes will have horns. No real accurate description can be accounted for due to the fact that usually no one survives when they see a wendigo.

Teakettlers - These creatures are said to be seen around lumberjack areas. They resemble a small dog that has stubby legs and ears like a cat. It only walks backwards. Steam and mist come out its mouth and makes a whistling sound that resembles a tea pot when boiling thus its name.

Hoop Snake - Said to be in Minnesota, North Carolina, and Wisconsin. This snake is said to be very aggressive and known to chase people. It will bite its own tail, form a circle or hoop, and roll towards its victim. Its venom is very poisonous.

Mississippi

Carrot top Aliens - On October 11th, 1973, two men in Pascagoul were abducted by aliens from another world and have unknown experiments done to them, the aliens were said to have red hair. One of the men whose name I will not mention has said to have continued encounters with this beings. Reports continue to this day throughout Mississippi of people encounter aliens from another planet. Some believe these beings keep returning to collect some type of information about humans while others believe that the space shipped crashed that day in October. After they conduction their experiments they received enough information in order to blend in with humans.

Mothman - On August 1 2007 the I35 w bridge crossing the Mississippi river collapsed. Killing 13 people and injuring 145 others.
It was said that a month prior sightings of a bird like creature was seen around this area. It wasn't until after the bridge collapsed that people believed it was the Mothman.

Mermaids of Pascagoula River - In 1982 there was an article posted in the times Picayune. It said that people reported of hearing flute like sounds coming from the river. It is believed that there are mermaids or a race of people that live beneath these waters. Some have claimed to have seen people walk both from the waters and walk into the waters only to disappear below. It is said that you can still hear this sound when the air is still.

Missouri

Ozark Howler - A cat like creature that lives in the Ozarks of Missouri. Has the body of a large black cat with stocky legs and sharp teeth. Some reports have said that is has horns while others say the ears resemble horns.

Momo - A large Bigfoot type creature that lives in the forests of Missouri. It is said to have piercing red eyes and log dark fur that covers its 7 foot tall humanoid body. Sights started in 1971.

Space Penguins - On February 14, 1967 a farmer in Tuscumbia claims that a space ship that resembled a mushroom landed in his field. As he approached this object, he noticed three foot tall figures waddling around the ship. They were green with black eye's. It is said that this farmer observed these beings for about five minutes before they went back into their ship and it took off.
Alien sights continue to this day in various parts of Missouri

Montana
Shunka Wara'kin also known as the Ringdocus was shot and killed in 1886 by Israel Ammon Hutchins on his ranch in Cameron, Montana.
This creature was known to sneak into Indian camps as well as various farms and steal dogs or other small animals to eat. The people of the area believed this was only one of kind creature but in 2006 new reports of this type of creature have been made. It is said to have killed over 120 various forms of livestock and wild life. These reports continue to this day.

   Werewolves - It is said that in the forest of Montana there are werewolves in the forests. Sounds of howling that are heard have been brushed off as regular wolves. These creatures are said to have the body of a man covered in fur but the head of a wolf with large claws for hands. The eyes are said to glow when anxious.

Nebraska

Jackalop - This legend is one of the most famous as well as humorous. It is not real but was created in this stated. It is a rabbit with horns.

Alkali Lake Monster - It is rumored that in this lake lives a large reptilian beast. The first report of the sighting of this creature was in 1923 and continue to this day.

Aliens - It is not known why but there are a rash of sightings in Nebraska. There are even beliefs that Aliens from outer space have taken up residency in this state. The most common sightings are of a diamond shaped crafts that shine brightly in the sky.
It is said that humanoid aliens with blond hair and blue eyes with a very smooth beautiful complexion are living in this state. It is not known if their ship has crashed or their true purpose of why they are living there.

Nevada

Giant fish of Lake Mead - Is was reported by divers in the 1990's that they saw a Giant fish in the waters. What they thought was a sewer pipe entrance was the mouth of Giant fish. Other swimmers and divers have also reported seeing a unusual giant fish in the lake. But reports have died down after the lake started to lower. It is believed this giant fish had swam up stream to a different area or that it got stuck in a drainage pipe.

The Roperite - The Roperite is a fearsome creature that is said to roam the Seirra Nevada Mountain range. Believed to have been hatched from an egg or just one of those mysterious of the desert. Its skin is a thick hide, has horns on its head, and flipper like feet. These feet give it the ability to jump high from rocks to other rocks. It's name comes from its beak which looks like a lasso that can wrap itself around its prey to devour.

Tesse - the lake monster. Similar to the lock ness monster. It is a giant serpent like creature that lives in the lake Tahoe. Its body is said to measure over 60 feet and have a thick barrel like body. Reports place three humps on its back. Sights go back to the early 1800's and continued through the 1970's.

Devil in the Desert - there is a rumor that people have spoke a man that can sometimes change shape into a devil like creature. He can appear and give you a piece of advice if he finds you interesting or fascinating in human form. There are some reports that deals have been made with him for wealth by the desperate in exchange for their souls. People who have done this only lose their lives a few years later usually in a gruesome manner. It is believed he comes for them in creature form.

Dragon of the desert - It is said that there is a dragon that can blend in with the rocks like a chameleon. Said to be the size of a car. Has large wings. Lives in a cave. Some believe that this dragon is protecting some ancient treasure.

 Hoodie - This is an urban legend that I just thought I would place in here. The legend is mostly known among the homeless. Hoodie is a dark figure that looks like a man that wears a black hoodie. This being has no face. Only darkness is seen when looked at the front of the hood. It is said that where ever there is an major accident, tragedy, or disaster the hoodie was either there or was seen just before there. If you see the hoodie also known as hoodman, get out of that area immediately.

Aliens and Area 51 - Nevada has been the talk of stories for a long time now about Aliens. It is because of the government area of land. Unusual sights have been seen in the desert and unusual creatures reported to be not of this world.

Strange creations - In the desert by the old nuclear test site it is said that there are many types of mutated animal and insect life. Ranging from half lizards and snakes to bizarre humanoid shaped beings that live in the desert area. The old timers of Nevada know not to venture out into certain parts of the desert because of these creatures.

New Hampshire

Wood Devils - This is an old lumber jack lore. The wood devils are large wood like creatures that are said to come from the trees. The have a humanoid shape and stand very tall with skin that resembles tree's. Lumber jacks that have been killed by fallen trees or other accidents around the tree's are blamed on these creatures. It was said that they were released by the cutting down of the tree's.

Dublin Lake monsters - In the 1980's a scuba diver reported seeing monsters that lived in a cave under the lake. He was so terrified of the experience he could not give descriptions without screaming in hysterics.

New Jersey

Jersey Devil - The Jersey Devil is a legendary creature that is said to inhabit the Pine Barrens of Southern New Jersey. It is a winged creature that has a humanoid body and hooves for feet. Reports of this creature have been made for the past 260 years by over 2000 people.

There are many colorful stories of what the creature is or where it comes from. One of the most popular is that a young woman that was cursed gave birth to one of the devils children.

Most popular sights of the Jersey Devil are :

- Joseph Bonaparte, former king of Spain and Brother of the famous Napoleon Bonaparte, reported seeing the Jersey Devil in Bordentown, NJ between 1816 and 1839 while out hunting.
- In the mid 1840's a strange creature with a piercing scream and odd hoof like foot prints began to kill live stock in the area around the Pine Barrens.
- January 16th 1909, Thack Cozzens of Woodbury, NJ, reported seeing a flying creature with glowing eyes flying down the street.
- January 16th 1909, In Bristol, PA, John Mcowen heard and saw the creature on the banks of a cannel.
- January 16th 1909, Patrol James Sackville fired on the creature as it flew away screaming.
- January 16th 1909, E.W. Minister, Postmaster for Bristol also reported seeing a bird like creature with a horse head, he reported that the creature also had a piercing scream.

January 18th 1909, one of the longest sightings of the Jersey Devil was reported by a Mr. and Mrs. Nelson Evans of Gloucester when they were awakened by a strange noise. Upon looking out the window, Nelson watched what he claimed to be the Jersey Devil for 10 minutes. Mr. Evans went on to describe the creature he saw that day: "It was about three feet and half high, with a head like a collie dog and a face like a horse. It had a long neck, wings about two feet long, and its back legs were like those of a crane, and it had horse's hooves. It walked on its back legs and held up two short front legs with paws on them. It didn't use the front legs at all while we were watching. My wife and I were scared, I tell you, but I managed to open the window and say, 'Shoo', and it turned around barked at me, and flew away."

January 16th 1909, a group of people in Camden, NJ, witnessed the Jersey Devil, upon spotting the people the Jersey Devil reportedly barked at them before taking off into the air and flying way.

January 19th 1909, a Burlington police officer and the Reverend John Pursell of Pemberton witnessed the Jersey Devil. Reverend John Pursell was quoted as saying "Never saw anything like it before".

January, 20th 1909, the Jersey Devil was witnessed by the Black Hawk Social Club and also seen by a trolley full of people in Clementon, NJ.

January 20th 1909, Mrs. Sorbinski of Camden heard a commotion in her back yard, upon inspection she discovered the Jersey Devil with her dog in its grasp, Mrs. Sorbinski, fearing for her dog's life, began to beat the Jersey Devil with a broom until it dropped her dog and flew off into the night.

January 21st 1909, Camden police officer Louis Strehr witnessed the Jersey Devil drinking from his horse's trough.

In 1927 a cab driver on his way to Salem suffered a flat tire, upon stopping to fix the flat an upright standing creature landed on the roof of his cab. The creature shook the cab violently, the cab driver ran from the scene, upon his return the creature was no where to be seen.

In 1961 a couple was parked in their car along a road in the Pine Barrens when they heard a load screeching noise outside. Suddenly the roof of their car smashed and the screeching sound was now right on top of them. The couple fled the scene but later returned to witness an unknown creature flying along the tree line making the same screeching noise.

In 1966 the Jersey Devil was blamed for the death of 31 ducks, 3 geese, 4 cats and two dogs at a local farm, one of the dogs was a large German Shepard found with its throat ripped out.

In 1987 in Vinland, NJ, another German Shepard was found torn apart and the body apparently gnawed upon, the body was located 25 feet from where the dog was chained up, around the body were strange unidentifiably tracks that no one could identify.

New Mexico

Gargoyles - Many reports of winged creatures that contain a humanoid body and large wings that are naked roam in the desert areas of New Mexico. These creatures have various types of grotesque facial features. Some have been seen with glowing red eyes.

Spring Heeled Devil - In the 1930's people of Silver city, reported seeing a well dress male wearing a cape jump to amazing heights and when he did let out a laugh that seem turned into a giggle to the on lookers.

Cactus Cat - The cactus cat is described as a bobcat like creature with thorn like fur and sharp boney type objects that go down its legs. Cowboys and Pioneers of the early 1900's reported seeing these animals. It is said that these creatures would come out at night and slash cactus and drink its sap. When it did it would become passive and leave passersby safe but if it was hunger would attack anyone nearby. Sounds of the creatures could be heard from the rubbing of the bony thorns that rub together on its legs.

New York

Kipsy - Also called the Hudson River Monster. First sighted in 1610.   It resembles a shark. Has a large body with sharp teeth.

Ratman - This is another urban legend amongst the homeless. It is said that there is a large creature about five feet tall with the body of a naked man with sharp nails on his long fingers, has the head of a rat and a long tail. This creature has been seen roaming the sewers and subway systems. Rarely will it go above and into the city. It will grab its victims and eat them alive. Sometimes only taking large bites.
It cannot speak but lets out a sound of that of a rat squealing.

North Carolina

Poop Monster - Blob like creatures that live in the sewer pipes of North Carolina. These creatures are not known what they do or even where they came from. Recently discovered and not much is known about them.

Lizard men of Lee County - The Lizard men have the body of a man that has scales over its entire green body, head of a lizard and a long tail. The hands and feet have only three claws. It was first believed that there was only one but many believe there are several.

North Dakota -

Devils lake monster - there are reports from 1894 and from Native American Legends speak of a large monster type creature that lives in the Lake. It has a large serpent like body and the head of a ferocious beast. Said to devour vessels that travel across the lake and people that swim in its waters. The lake is also known as the lake of spirits.

Ohio

There seems to be so much happening in the state of Ohio with the supernatural and monstrous   creatures as well as mysterious beings that I have decided to only list only a handful. With all the research I have done on this state I will be compiling it all in a future book that will be solely on Ohio. Hope you enjoy the few that I selected for you here.

Loveland Lake frog - In 2016, a couple spotted a frog type humanoid creature while walking. It had a humanoid type body with the head, hands and feet of a frog that stood four feet tall. A photo was taken by the couple but was deemed a fake however, they continue to insist that it is real.
However, reports have been sighted in that area of people and even the local police at the time at seeing frogmen since 1972.

Lady in White - It is said that in North Olmstead people have see a mysterious lady in white walking with a white flag at night. There are many stories but the real one is not known who she is. She will appear walking down the road and then seem to vanish into thin air.

Bessie the Lake Erie Monster - this is Cleveland's own loch Ness monster. Since 1892, reports of people seeing a large serpent like monster in Lake Erie. The sizes range from four feet to twenty feet long. It is said to have a brown serpent like body with a head that resembles a dinosaur. Some believe that the polluted waters keep this creature hidden from the world.

Mud Mermaids - Reports originated in Indiana and continue into Cincinnati. The heaviest of reports took place in 1894. Large amounts of half eaten animals and fish were found along the shores of the lakes. People claimed to have seen humanoid type creatures that looked as if they were covered in mud going into the water. At first people thought they were just people swimming but upon getting closer they noticed they had heads of creatures that resembled a cross between reptile and fish but had the bodies of human males with webbed fingers and large frog like feet.

Pumpkin head children - Reports of deformed children with heads that resembled large flesh colored pumpkins with dark terrifying eyes. The reports started in the 50's and continue to today. Most reports are in the Hinckley area but have also been though out Ohio. Some believe they are experiments that went wrong at a mental hospital that closed down while others believe they are some type of Aliens. These are different from the Melon head Children

Cemetery dwellers - Little creatures about 6 inches high have been seen living amongst the tree's in some local Cemeteries. They are said to have yellowish skin with large green eye's and a humanoid body. These creatures are sexless and have not defining features of either male or female. They are harmless and have been mainly seen by children. Children have said that they smile and wave, seem to project joy to the them.

Melon head Children - These creatures are the size of children with very large heads and shaped like melons. These creatures are said to be the creations of a Dr. Crow that injected unknown chemicals in the brains of his victims at a mental asylum during the 1970's. These chemicals caused their heads to expand and grow. It was not actually known what experiments the doctor was conducting.   After years of abuse these creatures killed the doctor, destroy his laboratory   and escaped into the woods. They are said to have violent tempers when hungry and have turned to cannibalism in order to survive during the cold winters. Eating the bodies of both the living and the dead. Only eating or attacking those that enter into their territory. They roam through the woods at night.

Apple Man - Only known to a handful. Pluck an apple from the tree and say that you give it to the apple man. It is not known who the apple man is but it is said that he brings blessings and good fortune to those who remember him especially in the season of autumn.

Green Man of Medina - Some have claimed to have seen a man peering at them through the trees and windows. This man is covered in leaves and arms that look like branches. The height is not known because he is usually crouched down amongst the lower bushes or piles of leaves. Some believe this being resides in an Amish farm and ventures out to the surrounding area's.

Oklahoma

Oklahoma Octopus - The secret of Lake Thunderbird. There have been reports of a large Octopus that lives in the lake, some say that the size range from the size of a horse to 30 feet.   It pulls its prey from the surface to the below into the lake. Said to have large teeth. Some have said the skin is deep green while others said it was black. It has been given the nickname, Okie the Octopus.

Ozark Howler - Also known as the Ozark Black Howler. This legendary creature is said to live in the remote parts of Oklahoma but has also been spotted in Texas and Arkansas. This creature is said to resemble a very large cat, about the size of bear. It has Thick black shaggy hair, Stocky legs, and horns on its head. Some have reported this creature to have several eye's while others only say that it has just two eyes.
It is also nocturnal and sleeps during the day. Some believe that before it sleeps it digs a hole in the ground beneath undergrowth while others say it seeks out shelter where it can. When it is on the prowl it howls like a wolf. It does this in search of others of its kind.

Oregon

Sasquatch - Also known as Bigfoot. This creature is said to be seven feet tall with a humanoid body, walks up right like a man and has hair covering its entire body.
He has been sighted in various woods throughout Oregon. There have been so many sightings that in some parts of the woods there are warning signs posted.
So far there have been no reports of this creature harming anyone. It runs away from the first signs of humans.

Lake Wallowa Monster - It is said that a large serpent with horns lives in this lake. It only raises its head above the water to look around and the vanish beneath the surface. Very little is known about this monster.

Colossal Claude - A Large serpent that was often sighted in the Columbia River. It was said to be 15 to 50 feet in length, have a horse-like head, tan colored skin, fins for arms, snake like body and a long tail. Reports were heavy around 1934 and slowly died off. In modern times there have been no reports of this creature.

Pennsylvania

The Squonk - A vicious creature that lives in the hemlock forests. It is said to always be unhappy and crying. It's true sorrow is not known but many suspect that it is from its ugly appearance, that it can't even to bear its own reflection others believe that it is in constant pain due to its mutation. Said to have baggy sagging skin, usually walks on all fours, a grotesque looking face and is covered with as many warts as it has moles. Believed to leave small puddles of tears in its path.
It is not wise to try and locate this creature for it is said to attack anyone that comes close to it.

Ogua - Located in the Monongahela river. Said to have the body of an alligator with the shell of a turtle. Some reports place it between 10 and 15 feet in length.

Devil like Creature - In 2000, there were several reports of the sightings of a strange creature. It was tall, thin, with spiky like arms and legs. It was all white skin and the head that resembled a dog or horse but the body of a man.

Rhode Island

Pawtucket Werewolf - Located in Pawtucket. It is said to be six feet tall, have the muscular body of a man, covered in fur or long black hair, a face that seems to that of both a mans and a wolf, long nails, and glowing eye's. Reports have been made for the past 30 years. It is rumored to be a man that transforms into this werewolf creature at certain times. It moves very fast through the woods.

South Carolina

Lizard Man of Scape Ore Swamp - This creature is said to be seven feet tall. Have a humanoid type body and walks upright. Has arms and legs but the head of a lizard. In the beginning of the sightings that began in the 1980's this creature has gone from being passive to being very aggressive. The latest reports in 2015, this creature was said to have attacking people and their cars. It is not known why it has now become so violent. If you see the lizard, Run !

The Grey man - It is not known if this is a spirit or some type of supernatural being. Some have even said that it is not of this world. It is a shadowy type being. Its features are hard to make out when seen but has the body of a man that looks out of focus. Reports go back to the early 1800's and continue to this day. Has been known to appear to people and give them messages of warnings of the future.

South Dakota

Iktomi - Dating by to the time of Native Americans that first lived in that area. It is said that this being is a trickster spirit. Can take on many forms. Sometime luring men to their deaths while others are merely tested on their own faiths and beliefs.

Tennessee

The whirling Whimpus - Resides in the mountains of
Cumberland. Some have also claim to have seen this creature in
other parts of Tennessee as well.
Said to stand seven feet tall and resemble a cross between a man
and a gorilla. It has enormous hands about three times the
normal size of a mans hands. Hooves for feet and walks on its
hind legs. It is said that this creature can move very fast, so fast
that it almost seems to appear invisible. Never leaves behind
any evidence.

Trolls - It is known throughout Tennessee of the trolls that seem
to be spotted throughout the state. They dress in clothing,
usually oversized and out dated. Short creatures. Look like men
but have hideous faces and lumps on their hands. Some are said
to have long hair.

The Bell Creature - In 1804, a creature was spotted by John Bell. It was said that the creature had the head of rabbit but the body of a dog with oversized claws. He tried to shoot the creature but was unable to and it vanished into the darkness of night. This creature continued to stalk him throughout his life and when he died, the creature disappeared. It is said that this creature will return to one of his descendants 107 years later

Texas

Chupacabra - These creatures are said to be all over the west but seem to be heavy in Texas. It is believed they originated in Mexico and some how came over into the USA.
They are about the size of dogs but have vicious teeth and move extremely fast. They are known to attack anything living for food. A cross between reptile and wild dog. Have tufts of matted hair and thick skin. Some people have said that their eyes glow red in the dark.

Big Bird - Reports of Giant bird type creatures have been going on since the old west. Many reports of these birds were in 1976. It was believed by some that it was a pterodactyl or a large bat. But no one was certain. What ever type of bird it was or is, is large enough to carry away a full size adult or animal. This bird is a meat eater.

Dust Devil - In swirling dust a black image has been seen. It resembles a man but no defining features. Resembles a shadow. Not much is known about this being but what is known is where ever it is seen disaster or hardships will follow in that area. He seems to be a link to an omen of something bad that will be happening soon.

Utah

Bear Lake Monster - A Mormon colonizer named Joseph C Rich, reported sightings of a creature in the Bear lake in the 1800's. The creature was said to be that of lizard but the head like an crocodile.   Some reports of sightings are still continued to this day.

Skin walkers - A skin walker is a shape shifter from a Native America legend. It is believed that these beings can take the shape of any form. There are various types of beliefs as to where these beings came from but the true nature is unknown. Even to this day there is talk that these beings exist.

There is a ranch called, Skinwalker ranch near Fort Duchesne and is said to be the home to many of these beings as well as other supernatural creatures. The ranch is believed to have highly unusual magnetic fields and areas that possess "dark energies". It has also be the sightings of otherworldly creatures and even Strange lights which some have said they are UFO.

Vermont

Champ - Lake Champlain is a long narrow body of water and within its waters is believed to be the home of the creature that is called, "Champ" also known by some as "Champy".
It is a large dark or black serpentine creatur that has a swan like neck on its serpent body with several humps on its back. It's head is said to resemble that of a sea-horse with three large teeth and yellow eye's. Sightings began in 1873, which PT Barnum offered a reward for the capture of this creature. Reports continue to this day.
It is believed to be fascinated by humans and tends to check out people. It is believed that this creature is harmless even though it has frighten many people that have encountered it.

This is one of the Monsters in the USA that are protected by Law. In 1982, the state of Vermont declared to pass a law to protect the creature from harm that lives in its waters.

Pigman - Pigman is said to lived in Northfield. It is described as a disturbing hybrid that is crossed between a pig and human. It has a human body with a pig head, distorted feet, naked, and covered in white hair. This creature is always reported to be violent if confronted. It can be found eating out of trash and garbage.
There is a rumor that back in 1951 a young boy named Sam Harris went missing due to demonic possession and because the possession took hold it turned him into this creature. While some reports believe it to be a medical experiment gone wrong. There are some that believe it is the offspring of someone that had sex with a pig. However, some just believe it is a man with mental disorders that wears a pig mask.

Virginia

Bunnyman Ghost - This story is one of ghost stories but I thought I would list it. Bunnyman is an urban legend in Fairfax County. In 1970, a man wearing a bunny suit or a some type of rabbit costume attacked people with an axe. It was said that he was walking along the Colchester overpass and was killed which many locals call it the bunnyman bridge. Many Believe that this killers spirit is trapped and bound to that bridge. It is said that if you go to the bridge at nigh you can see a ghostly shadow of the Bunnyman.

Since then strange mutilations of rabbits as well as other animals have been found in the area. Some missing persons and even murders have been credited to this being. The most powerful time for both activities and to see the bunnyman is at Halloween.

Washington

Seattle Sea Serpent - It was once believed that there was a serpent called willatuk. But it latter came out that this was a hoax created by Oliver Tuthill jr. He wanted to create his own legend based on combining information about the Loch Ness Monster with some Native American legends.

Batsquatch - April 19ᵗʰ, 1994, a report of a large 9 foot tall furry monster was on the road. It was is said to have blue tinted fur, a wolf like face, claws like a bird, Muscular arms and massive wings like a bat. As quickly as it appeared it vanished just as fast.
Bat like creatures like this have been reported being seen all over the world.

Snallygaster - A dragon like beast that has tentacles that come out of its mouth is said to inhabit the hills surrounding the state of Washington.

West Virginia

Mothman - Sightings of this creature or "Being" began in 1966 but some believe that Mothman has been around for even longer. This creature is said to be large in shape. It has been seen both as black and brown. Has large glowing red eyes. The body of a man with wings while others have said it resembled a large moth that stood on its hind legs. Said to be between 6 and 7 feet tall.

Where ever this creature has seen shortly after there is a major accident where there are many deaths. It is not known why this creature appears or what its purpose it. But it has many supernatural beliefs surrounding it.
Sightings are being reported all the time of this creature throughout West Virginia and even in parts of Virginia.

Grafton Monster - On the night of mid June of 1964, a reporter by the name of Robert Cockrell was driving him when he saw an obstruction in the road. As he approached it he noticed that it was actually something living. This creature had large white muscular body but no head was visible. Once seeing this he left quickly. He told others of this creature and returned with a couple of his friends to investigate and try to locate it. While searching the area a loud whistling sound was heard but there was no sight of this creature. The only thing that was found was a patch of grass that looked as if it was matted down from something that was once resting on it.
There were never any other reports of this creature again. It is believed that that this creature came from another dimension and some how returned.

Wisconsin

Hodag - It is said to live in the area of Rhinelander. Described as having a head of frog, face of an elephant, body of a lizard or dinosaur with short limps and a long spiky tail.
It's legend began in 1893 and even though a few people have tried to lay claim to its capture it is still believed to be alive.

Monona Monster - This legend has been around is the 1800's. It was first reported by a couple in a canoe. What they thought was a log that they bumped into was actually alive when they attempted to move it. No one has been able to get a clear view of it's actual shape but is said to have several tentacles.

Beast of Bray Road - Sighted in the 1980's on a rural road outside of Elkhorn. The creature is described as something similar to a werewolf with horns. Said to stand about 6 feet tall, have the from of a male that is covered in thick black hair, face that is a cross between a human and a wolf with large horns.

Wyoming

Smetty - In the Lake of DeSemt it is said that this is the home of a mysterious creature that reports have been made since the early 1800's. It is serpent type creature that is said to be approximately 30 feet long with the body as thick as a telephone pole.

Jack lope - A common folk tale that covers several states. It is said to that there is a rabbit with horns that resemble deer antlers and be able to jump at great heights.

www.ingramcontent.com/pod-product-compliance
Lightning Source LLC
Chambersburg PA
CBHW070036260726